Practical Mind-

A Course of Lessons on Thou
Telepathy, Mental-Currents, N

William Walker Atkinson

Alpha Editions

This edition published in 2024

ISBN 9789361479014

Design and Setting By

Alpha Editions

www.alphaedis.com

Email - info@alphaedis.com

As per information held with us this book is in Public Domain.
This book is a reproduction of an important historical work.
Alpha Editions uses the best technology to reproduce historical work
in the same manner it was first published to preserve its original nature.
Any marks or number seen are left intentionally to preserve.

Contents

LESSON I.	- 1 -
LESSON II.	- 5 -
THE CREERY EXPERIMENTS.	- 6 -
LESSON III.	- 11 -
LESSON IV.	- 16 -
GENERAL DIRECTIONS.	- 18 -
PRACTICE EXERCISE I. FINDING LOCATIONS.	- 20 -
PRACTICE EXERCISE II. FINDING LARGE OBJECTS.	- 21 -
PRACTICE EXERCISE III. FINDING SMALL OBJECTS.	- 21 -
PRACTICE EXERCISE IV. FINDING HIDDEN ARTICLES.	- 21 -
GENERAL REMARKS ON PRACTICE.	- 21 -
PREPARING FOR PUBLIC WORK.	- 22 -
LESSON V.	- 23 -
OPENING TALK.	- 23 -
CHOOSING THE TRANSMITTER.	- 23 -
INSTRUCTING THE TRANSMITTER.	- 24 -
BEGINNING THE TEST.	- 24 -
FINDING A LOCATION.	- 25 -
FINDING A PERSON.	- 25 -
FINDING A SMALL OBJECT.	- 25 -
FINDING A BOOK.	- 26 -
THE FLORAL TRIBUTE.	- 26 -
THE REUNITED COUPLE.	- 26 -
THE HIDDEN JEWELRY.	- 26 -

THE DISCOVERED COURSE.	- 27 -
REPLACING THE PIN.	- 27 -
THE THEFT DETECTED.	- 27 -
THE RECONSTRUCTED TABLEAU.	- 27 -
THE MURDER AND THE DETECTIVE.	- 27 -
THE RETURNED HATS.	- 28 -
THE LADY AND THE RING.	- 28 -
GENERAL ADVICE.	- 28 -
ABOUT TRANSMITTERS.	- 29 -
A WORD OF WARNING.	- 30 -
THE WIRE CONTACT.	- 30 -
THIRD PERSON INTERPOSED.	- 30 -
LESSON VI.	- 32 -
PRELIMINARIES.	- 32 -
DISCOVERING THE CARD.	- 32 -
THE CHECKER MOVE.	- 33 -
THE GAME OF CARDS.	- 33 -
THE MAPPED-OUT TRIP.	- 33 -
THE PACK OF CARDS.	- 34 -
THE CHOSEN WORD IN THE BOOK.	- 34 -
BLACKBOARD DEMONSTRATIONS.	- 35 -
DRAWING THE CHOSEN FIGURE.	- 35 -
THE LADY'S AGE.	- 36 -
THE BANK NOTE TEST.	- 36 -
THE WATCH NUMBER TEST.	- 36 -
THE GEOMETRICAL FIGURE TEST.	- 36 -
DRAWING PICTURES.	- 37 -

THE HIDDEN NAME.	- 37 -
THE UNDERLYING RULE.	- 37 -
THE "SIMPLER METHOD."	- 37 -
LESSON VII.	- 39 -
THE DRIVING FEAT.	- 39 -
THE COMBINATION LOCK FEAT.	- 39 -
THE OFFICE DETECTIVE FEAT.	- 40 -
THE POSTOFFICE FEAT.	- 40 -
THE FIRE-ALARM FEAT.	- 40 -
VARIATIONS.	- 41 -
"FAKE DEMONSTRATIONS" EXPOSED.	- 41 -
LESSON VIII.	- 42 -
THE FIRST STEPS.	- 43 -
DEMONSTRATIONS WITHOUT A TRANSMITTER.	- 43 -
EXERCISES FOR DEVELOPMENT.	- 43 -
REPRODUCING THE SPERRY FEATS.	- 44 -
THE WILLING GAME.	- 44 -
LONG DISTANCE EXPERIMENTS.	- 44 -
THE "AUTOMATIC WRITING" EXPERIMENTS.	- 45 -
THE STEAD EXPERIMENTS.	- 45 -
RAPPORT CONDITIONS.	- 46 -
THE BLACKBURN-SMITH EXPERIMENTS.	- 46 -
FINIS.	- 47 -

LESSON I.

THE NATURE OF MIND READING.

Only a few years ago the general public was in almost total ignorance of the great truth of Thought Transference, Thought Projection, Telepathy, or Mind Reading. It is true that here and there were to be found a few scientists earnestly investigating and eagerly uncovering the hidden truths concerning the subjects. But the mass of the people were either entirely ignorant of the subject, or else were intensely skeptical of anything concerning the matter, laughing to scorn the daring thinker who ventured to express his interest or belief in this great scientific phenomena.

But how different to-day. On all hands we hear of the wonders of Thought Transference, or Telepathy, as it is called. Scientific men write and teach of its fascinating manifestations, and even the general public has heard much of the new science and believes more or less in it, according to the degree of intelligence and knowledge concerning the subject possessed by the individual. Listen to these words from the lips of some of the greatest scientists of the day.

Prof. William James, the eminent instructor at Harvard University, says: "When from our present advanced standpoint we look back upon the past stages of human thought, whether it be scientific thought or theological thought, we are amazed that a universe which appears to us of so vast and mysterious a complication should ever have seemed to anyone so little and plain a thing. Whether it be Descartes' world or Newton's; whether it be that of the Materialists of the last century, or that of the Bridgewater treatises of our own, it is always the same to us—incredibly perspectiveless and short. Even Lyell's, Faraday's, Mill's and Darwin's consciousness of their respective subjects are already beginning to put on an infantile and innocent look." These remarks are doubly significant by reason of their having been made by Prof. James as the president of the "Society for Psychical Research."

The eminent English scientist, Sir William Crookes, in his address as president of the Royal Society, at Bristol, England, a few years ago, said: "Were I now introducing for the first time these inquiries to the world of science, I should choose a starting point different from that of old, where we formerly began. It would be well to begin with telepathy; with the fundamental law, as I believe it to be, that <u>thoughts and images may be transferred from one mind to another without the agency of the recognized</u>

<u>organs of sense</u>—that knowledge may enter the human mind without being communicated in any hitherto known or recognized ways. Although the inquiry has elicited important facts with reference to the mind, it has not yet reached the scientific stage of certainty which would enable it to be usefully brought before one of our sections. I will therefore confine myself to pointing out the direction in which scientific investigation can legitimately advance. If telepathy take place, we have two physical facts—the physical change in the brain of A. the suggestor, and the analogous physical change in the brain of B. the recipient of the suggestion. Between these two physical events there must exist a train of physical causes. Whenever the connecting sequence of intermediate causes begins to be revealed, the inquiry will then come within the range of one of the sections of the British Association. Such a sequence can only occur through an intervening medium. All the phenomena of the Universe are presumably in some way continuous, and it is unscientific to call in the aid of mysterious agencies when with every fresh advance in knowledge, it is shown that ether vibrations have powers and attributes abundantly equal to any demand—even the transmission of thought."

Prof. Crookes then went on to say: "It is supposed by some physiologists that the essential cells of nerves do not actually touch, but are separated by a narrow gap which widens in sleep while it narrows almost to extinction during mental activity. This condition is so singularly like that of a Branly or Lodge coherer (a device which has led Marconi to the discovery of wireless telegraphy) as to suggest a further analogy. The structure of brain and nerve being similar, it is conceivable that there may be present masses of such nerve coherers in the brain whose special function it may be to receive impulses brought from without through the connecting sequence of ether waves of appropriate order of magnitude. Roentgen has familiarized us with an order of vibrations of extreme minuteness compared with the smallest waves of which we have hitherto been acquainted, and of dimensions comparable with the distances between the centers of the atoms of which the material universe is built up; and there is no reason for believing that we have here reached the limit of frequency. It is known that the action of thought is accompanied by certain molecular movements in the brain, and here we have physical vibrations capable from their extreme minuteness of acting direct upon individual molecules, while their rapidity approaches that of the internal and external movements of the atoms themselves."

A formidable range of phenomena must be scientifically sifted before we effectually grasp a faculty so strange, so bewildering, and for ages so inscrutable, as the direct action of mind on mind. It has been said that nothing worth the proving can be proved, nor yet disproved. True this may have been in the past, it is true no longer. The science of our century has forged weapons of observation and analysis by which the veriest tyro may profit. Science has trained and fashioned the average mind into habits of exactitude and disciplined perception, and in so doing has fortified itself for tasks higher, wider and incomparably more wonderful than even the wisest among our ancestors imagined. Like the souls in Plato's myth that follow the chariot of Zeus, it has ascended to a point of vision far above the earth. It is henceforth open to science to transcend all we now think we know of matter, and to gain new glimpses of a profounder scheme of Cosmic Law. In old Egyptian days a well-known inscription was carved over the portal of the Temple of Isis: 'I am whatever has been, is, or ever will be; and my veil no man hath yet lifted.' Not thus do modern seekers after truth confront Nature—the word that stands for the baffling mysteries of the Universe. Steadily, unflinchingly, we strive to pierce the inmost heart of Nature, from what she is, to reconstruct what she has been, and to prophesy what she yet shall be. Veil after veil we have lifted, and her face grows more beautiful, august and wonderful with every barrier that is withdrawn.

Camille Flamarrion, the eminent French astronomer, is a believer in Thought Transference and Mind Reading, and has written the following expression of his convictions on this subject: "We sum up, therefore, our preceding observations by the conclusion that <u>one mind can act at a distance upon another, without the habitual medium of words, or any other visible means of communication</u>. It appears to us altogether unreasonable to reject this conclusion if we accept the facts. There is nothing unscientific, nothing romantic, in admitting that an idea can influence the brain from a distance. The action of one human being upon another, from a distance is a scientific fact; it is as certain as the existence of Paris, of Napoleon, of Oxygen, or of Sirius." The same authority has also said "There can be no doubt that our psychical force creates a movement of the ether, <u>which transmits itself afar like all movements of ether and becomes perceptible to brains in harmony with our own</u>. The transformation of a psychic action into an ethereal movement, and the reverse, may be analogous to what takes place on a telephone, where the receptive plate, which is identical with the plate at the other end, reconstructs the sonorous movement transmitted, not by means of sound, but by electricity."

We have quoted at length from this eminent authority to show once and for all that this great science of MIND-READING is recognized, and approved of by the highest authorities on Modern Science, and also to give our students the benefit of the current scientific theories upon the subject. In this work we have but very little to say about theory, but shall confine ourselves to facts, and actual instruction.

Science knows and has proven that thoughts may be and have been transmitted from one mind to another, in some cases over thousands of miles of space, but it has not as yet solved the mystery of the "Why" of the subject, and contents itself with explaining the "How." The nearest approach to a correct theory seems to be the one which compares the mind with the "wireless telegraph," and which supposes that the vibrations of thought travel through the ether, just as do the waves of this high order of electricity. The mind of one person acts like a "transmitter" of the wireless telegraph, while the mind of the other acts as a "receiver" of the same set of instruments.

There are undoubtedly vibrations set up in the brain when one thinks, and there are undoubtedly waves of thought just as there are waves of electricity. Science informs us that there is an increase of temperature in the human brain during periods of thought-activity, and also that there are constant chemical changes in the structure going on when the brain cells are active. This is akin to the generation of electricity in a battery, and undoubtedly acts in the same way in producing vibrations, and transmitting them to the brain of another. Sir William Crookes, in the address just quoted, points out the direction of the scientific theories concerning the matter. But, this is all that we shall have to say about the theory of Mind Reading. We shall now pass on to the actual practical instruction. The student is asked, however, to always carry in his mind the fact that Mind travels in waves from one brain to another just as electricity travels from the Transmitter to the Receiver. By holding this picture in your mind, you will have the whole practical theory, in condensed form, right before you, so that you may be able to act accordingly.

LESSON II.

THE PROOFS OF MIND READING.

As we have said in the previous chapter, the general public is gradually awakening to the knowledge of the reality of Mental Transference, and it is scarcely necessary to devote the time and space to a proof of the reality of the phenomena in these days, although a few years ago a work on the subject would have had to be composed principally of evidences and proofs. But, nevertheless, it may be well for us to take a hasty look at the nature of the proof in this work.

Nearly everyone has had evidences of Mind Reading or Thought Transference in his or her own life. Nearly every one has had experiences of being in a person's company when one of the two would make a remark and the other, somewhat startled, would exclaim, "Why, that's just what I was going to say," or words to that effect. Nearly every one has had experiences of knowing what a second person was going to say before the person spoke. And, likewise common is the experience of thinking of a person a few moments before the person came into sight. Many of us have suddenly found ourselves thinking of a person who had been out of our minds for months, or years, when all of a sudden the person himself would appear. These instances are so common as to be generally recognized, without question. These occurrences have given rise to the two common "sayings," viz., "Speak of the devil and his imps appear," or "Speak of angels and you hear the rustle of their wings."

Mark Twain, in an article printed several years ago, spoke of a plan that he had frequently practiced, i.e., that of writing a letter to a person upon some subject, then addressing the envelope and inserting the letter, and then tearing the whole thing into pieces instead of sending it. He stated that in a large percentage of such cases he would receive within a short time a letter from the person to whom the destroyed letter had been addressed, answering the questions asked, or else speaking along the same lines as those of the destroyed letter. We have known of this experiment being tried on people thousands of miles away from the writer, and also in cases in which the other person had not been heard of for many years. There is a field open for experiment along these lines which some of our students might investigate with profit and satisfaction.

Perhaps the best available evidence of Mind Reading at the disposal of the public to-day is that found in the records of the English Society for Psychical Research. The experiments of the members of this Society and other investigators have resulted in the piling up of a mass of facts more than sufficient to fully establish the correctness of the theory of Mind Reading. Series of carefully managed experiments have been conducted, the results of which have conclusively proven that the thought-waves set into motion by the mind of one person may be consciously received by the mind of another. We shall quote here from the reports of those investigators, in order to show you the important results that have been obtained, and to set at rest forever any lurking doubts as to the reality of the phenomena which may still find lodgment in your mind. Remember, please, that these committees were composed of some of the leading scientific authorities of England—men whose standing and reliability, as well as whose judgment, was beyond question. These cases form a part of the scientific records of the English Society.

THE CREERY EXPERIMENTS.

One of the interesting series of experiments conducted by members of the English Society was that of the family of the Rev. A.M. Creery, of Derbyshire, England. This investigation was made upon hearing the report of the Rev. Mr. Creery regarding a number of experiments he had conducted with his four children. He reported that he had begun by practicing a variation of what is generally known as the "willing game", in which one of the party leaves the room, and the company selects some object to be hidden, after which the person is recalled to the room when the company concentrates its mind upon the hidden object, and the seeker eventually finds it by means of Mind Reading. The reverend gentleman said in his report to the Society:

"We began by selecting the simplest objects in the room; then chose names of towns, people, dates, cards out of a pack, lines from different poems, etc., any thing or series of ideas that those present could keep before the mind steadily. The children seldom made a mistake. I have seen seventeen cards chosen by myself, named right in succession without any mistake. We soon found that a great deal depended upon the steadiness with which the ideas were kept before the minds of the thinkers, and upon the energy with which they willed the ideas to pass. I may say that this faculty is not confined to the members of one family; it is much more general than we imagine. To verify this conclusion I invited two of a neighbor's children to join us in our experiment, and very excellent results we secured from them."

The Society then began a series of careful investigations extending over a period of one year. The utmost care was taken to obviate the chance of fraud, collusion, mistakes, or outside influences. The experiments were conducted partly in Mr. Creery's house and partly in rooms selected by the members of the investigating committee. Having selected at random one of the children, the child would be taken from the room and accompanied by a member of the committee would wait out of sight or hearing of the room. The remainder of the committee would then select a card from a pack, or else write down a name or number which occurred to them at the moment. The following verbatim report of what followed will give you an idea of the results generally obtained. The report goes on to say:

"On re-entering the room the little girl would usually stand with her face to the wall, placed thus by us. But sometimes she would stand with her eyes directed toward the ground for a period of silence varying from a few seconds to a minute, till she called out to us some number, card or what it might be." The report states that in the case of giving the names of objects chosen, the child scored six cases out of fourteen. In the case of naming of small objects held in the hands of members of the committee, she scored <u>five out of six</u>. In the case of naming cards she scored six out of thirteen. In the case of stating fictitious names chosen by the committee she scored, at a first trial, five out of ten.

One of the experiments is reported as follows:

"One of the children was sent into an adjoining room, the door of which was closed. The committee then thought of some object in the house and wrote the name down on paper. The strictest silence was observed. We then all silently thought of the name of the thing selected. In a few seconds the door of the adjoining room opened, and the child would appear <u>generally with the object selected</u>. No one was allowed to leave the room after the object had been fixed upon; no communication with the child was conceivable, as her place was often changed. Further, the only instructions given to the child were to fetch some object in the house that we would fix upon and would keep in mind to the exclusion of all other ideas. In this way we wrote down, among other things, a hairbrush—it was brought; an orange—it was brought; a wine-glass—it was brought; an apple—it was brought," etc., etc.

The report to the Society sums up the following results: Three hundred and eighty-two trials were made in the series. In the test of naming the chosen letters of the alphabet, cards, and numbers of two figures, the chances against the girl were 21 to 1, 51 to 1, and 89 to 1, respectively. In the case of stating chosen surnames the odds against her were very much in excess of the figures just named. In the cases of the experiments of naming chosen cards it was calculated that a mere "guesser," according to the law of probability, would be able to correctly name <u>but seven and one-third</u> out of a total of the three hundred and eighty-two trials. The actual results obtained by the child were as follows: On the first attempt, <u>one hundred</u>

and twenty-seven; on the second attempt, fifty-six additional; and on the third attempt, nineteen additional—making a grand total of two hundred and two successes out of a possible three hundred and eighty-two! On one occasion five cards straight running were successfully named on a first trial. The mathematical chances of a mere "guess" doing this feat, under the Law of Average, or Probabilities, are estimated at over a million to one against the chance. And this was not merely an isolated, exceptional case, for there were other "long runs"; for instance, there were two cases in which runs of eight straight consecutive successes were scored, once with names, and once with cards. In the case of the eight consecutive cards it has been figured that the chances against the girl would figure up at least 140,000,000 to 1, according to the Law of Average and Probabilities. To understand just what this means it may help you if you will think that the feat was like picking out one chosen man in a population of one hundred and forty millions, nearly double the population of the United States. And yet there are people who would dismiss matters like this with the remark, "mere coincidence"!

The interest in the Creery children attracted the notice of Prof. Balfour Stewart, LL.D., and Fellow of the Royal Society. This distinguished gentleman testifies as follows:

"In the first instance, when I was present, the thought-reader was outside a door. The object or thing thought of was written on paper and silently handed to the company in the room. The thought-reader was then called in, and in the course of perhaps a minute the answer was given. Definite objects in the room, for instance, were first thought of, and in the majority of cases the answers were correct. These numbers were thought of and the answers were generally right, but, of course, there were some cases of error. The names of towns were thought of, and a good many of these were right. Then fancy names were thought of. I was asked to think of certain fancy names and mark them down and hand them around to the company. I then thought of, and wrote on paper, 'Bluebeard,' 'Tom Thumb,' 'Cinderella,' and the answers were all correct."

Subsequent experiments with the Creery children, at the house of the well known investigator, Mr. F.W.H. Myers, at Cambridge, England, proved equally successful. The children, and their ages, were as follows: Mary, 17; Alice, 15; Maud, 13. The percentage of successes obtained at Mr. Myers' house tallied very well with those obtained elsewhere. One remarkable result was obtained, though, that had not been obtained before. On one occasion the child was asked to name the "suit" of cards chosen one after another. That is, of course, the child was asked to name which suit, "hearts," "diamonds," "clubs" or "spades," were shown of the card drawn and seen by the committee, and then thought of. On this occasion the child scored a run of <u>fourteen straight running, consecutive successes</u>. The chances against this success were 4,782,969 to 1.

We will close by mentioning another remarkable series of experiments conducted by the same Society. The Mind Reader was M.G.A. Smith, of England. Among other startling feats successfully performed by Mr. Smith, that of the reproduction of Geometrical Figures was perhaps the most remarkable. In this feat Mr. Smith sat blindfolded, in a room belonging to the committee, with a pad of paper before him and a member of the committee on each side of him. A selected member of the committee then would go outside of the room, and behind a closed door would draw some geometrical figure at random. Returning to the room the figure would be shown to the committee, and also to Mr. Douglas Blackburn, who acted as the Transmitter for Mr. Smith, the latter being known as the Receiver. The Transmitter, with closed eyes, now took his position immediately back of Mr. Smith, but at a distance of two feet from him, no contact being allowed, this precaution being taken to obviate charges of confederacy, etc. The Transmitter would then concentrate his mind intently for a few minutes, and in a short time Mr. Smith would receive the impression of the mental image in the mind of the Transmitter, and would begin to attempt to reproduce it on paper. In the series of experiments running over a period of four days thirty-seven drawings were made, of which only eight were considered unsuccessful. <u>Twenty-nine successes out of a possible thirty-seven, remember.</u>

The committee reports that it took all the precaution to guard against secret signals, etc., and that confederacy, fraud, collusion, or similar methods were out of the question. The eight cases of failure consisted of four cases in which Mr. Smith received no impression, and therefore could not reproduce the drawing; and four cases in which the drawing was so vague and imperfect as to be called a total failure. Some of the figures were grotesque, unusual, and complicated, but all were reproduced in a more or less perfect manner. The drawing was made deliberately and without hesitation, and as if Smith had actually seen the figure shown to the Transmitter a few moments before. On one occasion, in order to be doubly guarded against collusion, they closed Mr. Smith's ears with putty, tied a bandage around his eyes and ears, pulled a bolster-case over his head, and then covered him all over with a blanket which completely enveloped his body and head. <u>And under these extraordinary conditions he reproduced the figures with his usual success.</u>

We could proceed relating case after case, experiment after experiment, conducted by these scientific bodies of learned and careful men. But the story would be no more convincing than that related above. And, after all, there is a method of satisfying yourself that is far more conclusive than the reading of any results of experiments of others—and that is to learn to perform the feats of Mind Reading yourself. By means of a very little practice you will be able to reproduce many of the demonstrations of the public performers, as well as the experiments of the scientific societies, and then when you have realized that you can do these things you will need no further proof of the reality of the science of Mind Reading.

LESSON III.

"CONTACT" MIND READING.

Mind Reading is divided by the authorities into two general classes, viz., "Contact" Mind Reading and "Telepathic" Mind Reading.

The first of these classes, "Contact" Mind Reading, is demonstrated by physical contact between the Transmitter (or active agent) and the Receiver (or passive agent) in order to afford an easy channel for the passage of the vibrations, thought-waves, nerve-currents, or magnetism of the Transmitter (according to the several theories favored by scientists). The second class, "Telepathic" Mind Reading, is demonstrated by the transferral of the "waves," "vibrations," "currents," or "magnetism" of the Transmitter to the Receiver over the ether, through space (often for thousands of miles) without the more convenient "wires" of the nerves of the two agents.

You will readily see that two classes of phenomena closely resemble the two classes of telegraphic phenomena, i.e., the "wire" system and the "wireless" system. There is a striking analogy between electric phenomena and mental force phenomena all the way through the subject, and this subject of Mind Reading is simply one of the many forms of the resemblance.

We shall begin by giving you instructions in the first form—Contact Mind Reading, as it is the simplest and most easy of accomplishment and demonstration. And besides, the best Telepathists have been trained by means of the practice of Contact Mind Reading at the start. One leads to the other, just as the ordinary wire telegraph naturally led to the "wireless" system, which is even now but in its infancy.

At this point we wish to point out to you a most grievous error, and unjust judgment, that certain so-called scientists and investigators have fallen into regarding this matter of Contact Mind Reading. In order to give you a clearer idea of the nature of this error, we must call your attention to the fact that Contact Mind Reading has been given much publicity through the advertisements and performances of several celebrated public performers, and their lesser-light imitators.

These performers, like many others, have sought to give an attractive public entertainment rather than a scientific demonstration, and some of them have found it much easier to "fake" some of the demonstrations rather than to perform them according to scientific principles. And the careful investigators soon discovered that in certain cases there was no

Mind Reading at all, but only a clever imitation which was styled "Muscle Reading." In other words, instead of the performer receiving his mental impressions from the mind of the Transmitter, over the nervous system of other persons, he would push up against him, and by a clever system of pushing, pulling, leading, and leaning would detect the muscular movements of the Transmitter, and by careful practice would learn to interpret these movements so as to get an indication of the location of the hidden objects and practically be led or pushed toward the spot. But even in these cases, the performer would of necessity have to employ more or less genuine Contact Mind Reading to finish the feats. The only advantage the performer gained by resorting to these unfair methods was that it was less fatiguing to his mind and enabled him to "fake" through the performance with less mental wear and tear.

The investigators, easily discovering the above mentioned "faking" performances, came to the conclusion that the whole thing was a "fake," and could be explained by the "muscle reading" theory entirely. And so the news was spread broadcast, and you will find a number of books written explaining Contact Mind Reading on this hypothesis. Of course some of the public may prefer to accept this erroneous theory, but we wish to say here positively that if any person will honestly investigate for himself, and will learn to make the demonstrations personally, he or she will soon discover that "muscle reading" has nothing to do with the genuine phenomena. The proof of the thing is in the doing of it, and you may learn the truth for yourself if you will but try the feats and demonstrations, herein given, just as we teach them. The result of such practice will cause you to feel with us the indignation arising from the attempts to belittle a noble scientific principle, and practice, by an explanation arising from the witnessing of "fake" imitations of the real thing.

The truth is that the muscles have nothing to do with the passage of the mental currents or waves from the Transmitter to the Receiver any more than they have to do with the transmission of nervous sensations from body to brain, or the motor impulses from brain to body. When you wish to close your hand you send a nervous current from your brain to the muscles controlling your hand. The current travels along the nervous system, and is by it distributed over the muscles causing them to contract. A current from a galvanic battery will cause the muscles to act in the same way. But the muscle is the machinery affected and set into motion, and the nerves are the delicate telegraphic wires leading to the parts.

And so it is with this transmission of the mental waves and currents. The brain of the Transmitter, aroused by his active Will, sends a powerful current or wave through his nervous system. When it reaches the extremity of his fingers it leaps over the tiny space separating his nerves from the nerves of the Receiver, and enters the nervous system of the latter, and influences his actions. The Receiver being in a passive condition, and his brain sending practically no impulses over his nerves, he is in a receptive condition to the imparted nervous current, which acts upon him something like an impulse from his own brain, only weaker. That is the whole secret of Contact Mind Reading. It is "Nerve Reading" if you like, but certainly <u>not</u> Muscle Reading.

The tips of the fingers of a person of fine sensibilities, and delicate touch, are known by anatomists to be filled with masses of nerve-matter similar to that forming parts of the brain. In fact they are tiny finger-brains, and they will send out, convey, and receive delicate impulses from one mind to another. Those of you who have experienced the peculiar touch of some persons of this kind, can bear witness to the fact that a subtle "magnetism" or current passed from them to you. This is a fact well known to investigators of psychic phenomena, and such people laugh at the crude "muscle reading" theories, for they have disproved them repeatedly in actual careful experiments. And you may do the same, if you will practice the demonstrations given in this book. The fact that the developed Contact Mind Reader usually walks ahead of his Transmitter, instead of being led by him; and that he usually allows the latter's arm to hang limp, instead of muscularly contracted, is another proof of the absurdity of the theory above mentioned. Besides this, wires may be used between the two persons, or even a third person may be placed between them. But, as we have said, after all the best and only real test is to try the experiments yourself and learn that "muscle reading" has nothing to do with the real phenomena.

The experimenter will soon find that when he gets into the work and is engaged in a search for a hidden object, by means of Mind Reading, he will forget all about the Transmitter. He will almost forget where he is, and will feel himself floating and gliding over the floor and scarcely touching it with his toes. He will find himself drawn or impelled irresistibly toward the hidden object, as if by some outside energy or fine force. He will feel the hidden object <u>drawing him like a magnet</u>, and attracting him to the spot. He will forget his audience, and everything else, in his desire to reach the Centre of Attraction. These experiences cannot well be explained in print, but the investigator will soon learn to know them for himself, and he will be amazed and filled with wonder at the strange psychical phenomena in which he is taking a principal part.

And, then, and then only will he be able to intelligently reject the absurd and unjust theories of "muscle reading," and to see the crudeness of the attempted explanation. He will see that the foolish theory is as far out of the way as the ignorant person's idea that the telegraph messages are sent by the wires being "pulled" or "jerked," instead of being but channels for the passage of the electric fluid, or magnetic waves. He will class such pretended scientists with those "doubting Thomases" who, when gas was first introduced in the British House of Parliament, insisted that the pipes rendered the building unsafe, because they would become heated by the passage of the light; and who when the system was seen in actual operation, would gently feel the pipes with their gloved fingers, wondering why they felt no heat. We trust that we have said enough to convince you of the ridiculousness of the "muscle reading" theory, and to give you sufficient interest to demonstrate the matter for yourself.

Many of our readers have witnessed the public performances of the several well-known "Contact" Mind Readers who have visited the leading cities of this country and other lands. Of course, the average public performer soon discovers that the average patron of his performance attends principally to be amused, and entertained, rather than to be instructed. And he is apt to gradually add sensational features to the performance, for the purpose of thrilling and mystifying the audience, knowing that by so doing he will better please his patrons than if he were to give them a strictly scientific demonstration of the science of Contact Mind Reading as produced in the psychological laboratories of the great investigators of the subject. Some of these public performers have even gone so far as to add "fake" features to their performance, employing confederates, and in other ways introducing unscientific methods in order to intensify the interest and satisfaction of their audiences.

But notwithstanding this fact, the average public Mind Reader, in spite of his sensational additions, generally gives his audience enough of "the real thing" to render his performance of sufficient scientific interest to make it worthy of attendance by the earnest student of the subject. And we believe that the time is approaching when a strictly scientific performance will prove of sufficient interest to the public to render it worth while for a new class of entertainers and lecturers to arise and take the field, instructing the public regarding their great subject and illustrating their theories by striking experiments along scientific lines. And we think that this little book will do its part in the direction of educating the public mind to appreciate such an entertainment, as well as serving to educate future entertainers for their life work.

However, in this little book, we shall treat the subject as if a parlor demonstration was all that is desired, and our instructions and directions shall be chiefly toward that end, although we wish to say that any man or woman who will carefully study these instructions and directions, and who will carefully practice the feats and exercises, will be able to gradually develop sufficient ability and skill to give a successful public performance, and perhaps reap a goodly share of fame and financial reward. The principles of the parlor demonstration, and the public performance are the same. These same instructions and directions have been studied and applied by some of the best performers now before the public, illustrating the wonders of Contact Mind Reading. So that if any of the students of this work have ambitions in the direction of public performance, they will find herein the methods calculated to develop them into a successful public entertainer and demonstrator.

Anyone may develop himself, or herself, into a good Contact Mind Reader by practice, and perseverance. As in everything else in life, some will succeed better than others; and some will find the work easier than do others, but all may develop quite a respectable degree of proficiency in a short time. A little careful, conscientious practice and experiment will accomplish wonders.

Mind Reading feats depend upon the degree of Will and Concentration on the part of the Transmitter, and upon the degree of Receptivity and Passivity upon the part of the Receiver. We are taking it for granted that the student will wish to act as a Receiver (or Performer of the feat of Mind Reading) rather than as the Transmitter (or person called upon to have his mind read). And so we shall address him as such, with this understanding. But we shall also give herein full directions for the Transmitter, as well, in order to give the student the methods necessary to act in either capacity, and to also enable him to instruct the Transmitter in his work. The Receiver should understand the duties of the Transmitter, in order that the best possible results be obtained, and the proper harmony and <u>rapport</u> conditions may be established.

LESSON IV.

DEVELOPMENT EXERCISES.

The student should practice privately with the assistance of a few friends, before he ventures before a parlor audience, for by so doing he overcomes the first lack of confidence in himself, and the awkwardness natural to the beginner along any new line of work. By careful and repeated practice he gains confidence in himself by reason of his growing success in his experiments, and besides wears off the "rough edges" of his actions, etc., so that when he finally appears before an audience he will feel perfectly self-possessed and at ease, and thus be able to devote his entire attention to his work, without annoying self-consciousness and awkwardness.

Begin the Development Exercises by selecting one or more friends who are in sympathy with you, and who are interested in the subject. Do not have any unsympathetic or uncongenial persons around when you are practicing, for such people tend to distract your attention from your work, and really exert a detrimental effect upon the preliminary work. Select one of your friends as the Transmitter and take the part of the Receiver yourself.

Begin your practice by establishing a Psychic Harmony, or Rapport, between yourself and your Transmitter by means of Rhythmic Breathing. Although this feature of the work has been overlooked by many investigators of the subject, still it is a very important feature of the work, and one that is conducive to the production of the very best results along these lines of psychic demonstrations.

The term "Rapport" is one frequently met with in occult and psychic books. The word is defined by Webster as "Relation; conformity; correspondence; sympathetic accord." It is used by occultists in the sense of: "having harmonious vibrations with another," the occult teachings being that every person has his or her own rate of mental vibration which, when in harmonious accord with the vibrations of another, induces the most favorable conditions for the production of mental or psychic phenomena, or mental relations; sympathetic understanding, etc. This "harmonious vibration" does not necessarily mean that the two persons must be attuned to precisely the same key, but that their keynotes must harmonize, instead of producing discord. The comparison of the notes of the musical scale will illustrate the principle thoroughly. When two persons are in "rapport" with each other, there is a mental and psychic harmony between them, which is productive of the best possible mental co-operative work. Hence the necessity of good rapport conditions in Mind Reading.

Rhythmic Breathing has been known to occultists of all ages as one of the important adjuncts of Psychic Phenomena, and its use in bringing about Rapport Relations is thoroughly understood by all Practical Occultists. Rhythmic Breathing consists in the person breathing in slow measured regular rhythm. It may be acquired by counting the indrawn breath, the retained breath, and the outgoing breath, by regular beats like the ticking of a large clock. For instance, draw in your breath slowly, counting mentally according to the ticking of an imaginary large clock: "one—two—three—four." Then hold the breath, counting "one—two." Then breathe out slowly: "one—two—three—four." The rule is that the indrawn breath should have the same number of counts as the outgoing breath, the held-breath taking up but one-half the counts of either of the others. The above count illustrates this matter. The advanced occultists get their time-beat from the pulse-beats, but this is not absolutely necessary in this connection. The principal point about Rhythmic Breathing that we wish to impress upon you now is that the two persons, the Transmitter and Receiver, should breathe in unison with each other—that is in perfect time and rhythm. This breathing in unison will soon establish the very best possible rapport conditions between them. From four to seven Rhythmic Breaths will be sufficient to establish the proper conditions in ordinary cases. In the performance of a test, in case you should feel the power of the Transmitter failing, you should stop and ask him to breathe in unison with you for a moment, and then re-start your work. By breathing a little loud the other person will catch your time, so that it is not necessary for you to instruct him in the science or theory of Rhythmic Breathing. Simply tell him to breathe in unison, and keeping time with you.

Begin all your practicing with this Rapport Breathing, and start each demonstration with it, also. You will find that it will have a very soothing, calming, quieting effect upon both persons, and will produce in each a mental earnestness and concentration that will help along the demonstration of Mind Reading.

We shall not mention this Rhythmic Breathing or Rapport Condition when we proceed to give you the detailed direction, for the demonstration, but you must remember that it should be observed in each case. Of course, you will be able to get results without it—but not so easily, or so thoroughly and satisfying.

It is well to conclude your practice by taking a few deep breaths by yourself, and not in unison with the Transmitter. This destroys the Rapport Condition.

GENERAL DIRECTIONS.

The prime requisite for a successful demonstration of Mind Reading is the acquirement, or possession, by the Transmitter, of a clear idea of <u>direction</u> in his mind. The associated requisite is that the Transmitter be able to <u>concentrate his will</u> upon the mind of the Receiver, impressing upon him the <u>Sense of Direction</u> so strongly that he will move in accordance with the Will of the Transmitter. Remember the two points to be observed by the Transmitter.

Begin by having the Transmitter standing beside you in the centre of the room, <u>you being blindfolded</u>. Have him mentally select some one corner of the room, saying nothing to you of his choice. Then let him concentrate his mind upon that one corner, forgetting every other part of the room. Then have the Transmitter grasp your Left Hand with his Right Hand, you grasping his fingers in your hand and lifting the hand to your forehead. Hold the hand against your forehead, just above your eyes. Instruct him then to <u>will</u> that you go to the corner of the room that he has selected, shutting out all other thoughts from his mind, and <u>concentrating</u> his entire Attention upon the projection of his Will. He must not content himself merely forming a Mental Picture of the selected corner, but must think of the <u>Direction</u> of that corner, just as he would in case he were to wish to walk there himself. He must not simply think "That Corner"—he must think "<u>There!</u>" using the sense of Direction. He must <u>will</u> that you shall <u>go there</u>, carrying the words "<u>Go There!</u>" in his mind.

You, the Receiver, must place yourself in a perfectly <u>passive</u> and <u>receptive</u> state of mind, resigning your own Will for the time being, and being perfectly willing and desirous of being mentally <u>directed</u> or <u>led</u> by the Will of the Transmitter. He is the Active factor, and you the Passive. It is the strength of his Will, and the degree of your Receptivity that makes the demonstration a success.

Keep your eyes closed, even though you be blindfolded, for by so doing you induce a Passive state of mind, and even the stray glimpses that you may catch through the handkerchief will serve only to distract you. You must shut out sights, and even thought of sights.

Stand quiet a moment or two, awaiting impressions from the mind of the Transmitter, who is making the mental command: "<u>Go there; go there, I say!</u>" while at the same time he is <u>willing</u> that you follow his command.

After a moment or two of passive and receptive waiting, you will begin to feel an impulse to move forward. Obey this impulse and take the first step, which will often be in an entirely opposite direction from the selected corner. The idea of this first step is to "get started." While you are taking the first step or two, you will feel a clearer impulse toward the real selected corner, and will find yourself swinging around to it. Do not grow impatient, for you are but learning to receive the impressions. Advance one foot forward, hesitatingly, resting your weight on the ball of the other foot, and you will soon feel yourself being <u>compelled</u> to move in a certain direction, which will end in your moving toward the right corner. You will soon become conscious of being directed by the <u>Will</u> of the Projector, whose mind is acting upon yours and leading and directing you toward the right place.

It is difficult to describe to you the exact feeling that you will experience, but a little practice will soon make it clear to you. Follow the impulse, and you will soon begin to feel the mental command, "This way—this way—no, not that way but <u>this way</u>," until you will reach the desired spot, when you will feel the command: "That's right—stop where you are—this is the place." If you start to wander off in the wrong direction you will begin to feel the correcting impression: "<u>This way—this</u> way, I tell you," and if you will but passively receive and follow the mental telegraph message you will find the impulse growing stronger and stronger until you walk right into the corner selected, when you will feel that you have "reached Base," as the children say in their games. When you walk in the right direction you will feel the mental message, "Right, right you are"; and when you move in the wrong direction you will feel the mental message, saying "No, no, not that way—<u>This way</u>, I say, come along, <u>come</u>!" By practice you will soon become quite sensitive to these guiding thought-waves, and will act upon them almost automatically. Practice will soon so sharpen your perceptive faculties that you will often be able to move right off to the desired corner at once, sometimes actually running right to it, dragging the Transmitter after you.

You will soon begin to notice that there is quite a difference in the power of Concentration on the part of different people acting as the Transmitter. Some will be able to Concentrate so forcibly that they will send you the message clear and sharp, while others will send only a feeble and wavering message. The more Concentration the Transmitter has the stronger will be the message. It will be very advisable for you to experiment with a number of persons acting as the Transmitter, so that you may become familiar with the different degrees of Concentration, personal characteristics of people in Transmitting, etc. This will aid you when you begin your parlor performances.

When you find a lazy Transmitter who is sending only feeble messages, you must remonstrate with him, telling him that he must exercise his <u>Will-Power</u> more. This plan will often arouse in them a desire to give a good exhibition of their Will-power, and they will begin sending you strong mental impulses. It is a good plan, when you have an unsatisfactory Projector, to extend his arm out its full length and hold it up about the height of your eyes. In this way he feels the strain, and it arouses his Will in order to hold it there, which seems to act in the direction of his sending sharper and clearer messages and impulse. In case the Transmitter proves very unsatisfactory, substitute another for him. But as a rule this unsatisfactoriness arises from the fact that he does not fully understand his duties—does not know what is required of him. A little practice and instruction will bring him out all right. It is often advisable to let the Transmitter read this book of instructions, if he happens to be a personal friend who is helping you out in your practicing and experiments. The Transmitter will find that by <u>looking</u> toward the selected corner, he will be aided in concentrating his attention and directing his Will Power.

Practice this exercise and experiment, in different rooms, and with different Transmitters, until you can go readily to the selected corner. Do not be discouraged, but remember that "practice makes perfect," and that like any other thing the art must be learned by patient practice and repetition. It is like learning to play the violin—skating—dancing, or anything else. If after a number of trials you begin to feel tired, stop practicing and adjourn the experiments until the next day. Do not unduly strain yourself, or tire out your mind. When the next day comes you will be surprised at the added proficiency you have gained.

You may vary the above method by holding the Transmitter's hand out at arm's length, instead of holding it up to your head. Some find one plan more effective, and others prefer the second. The principle is the same in both cases, so adopt either plan, or any variation thereof, providing it proves effective.

PRACTICE EXERCISE I. FINDING LOCATIONS.

After you have grown proficient in locating the corners of rooms, you may have the Transmitter select other parts of the room, such as doors, mantels, windows, alcoves, projections, etc. Try a number of these selected locations in turn, gaining a variety of experiences which will prove valuable later on. In all of these experiments the Transmitter must guard you from running into obstacles, furniture, etc., by telling you to avoid them, guiding you past them, and in other proper ways prevent you from bruising yourself or breaking or upsetting things. You must impress this upon his mind, and then you should give yourself into his care with the utmost confidence, giving yourself no further concern about these things, and keeping your mind as passive as possible. Don't allow your mind to be distracted by outside things—attend to the matter of the experiment in which you are engaged.

PRACTICE EXERCISE II. FINDING LARGE OBJECTS.

The next step should be the selecting and finding of large objects in the room, such as chairs, tables, etc. Proceed as in the previous exercises. Do not neglect this exercise in your desire to do more wonderful things, for you need just this training. You will realize the importance of these exercises after you begin to appear before friends and evening companies, etc., when you will be called upon to find hidden objects, selected articles secreted under tables, on persons, on furniture, etc. If you can find selected chairs you will be able to more readily find persons seated on chairs. Continue this exercise until you can readily find any and every piece of furniture in a room, and the other large objects in a room as well, when they are thought of by the Transmitter.

PRACTICE EXERCISE III. FINDING SMALL OBJECTS.

After mastering the above exercise have the Transmitter select some small articles, such as a book, vase, ornament, etc., on a table, mantel-piece, etc. Proceed as before, varying the objects and places, endeavoring to get as wide a range of experiences as possible along the line of Mind Reading of this kind.

PRACTICE EXERCISE IV. FINDING HIDDEN ARTICLES.

After you have mastered the last mentioned exercise, have the Transmitter select a small object, such as a watch-key, match-safe, etc., and secrete it in some part of the room, you remaining out of the room until the article is selected and hidden. Proceed as before, until you find the secreted object. Your Transmitter should endeavor to give you a great variety in this exercise, in order to properly train you for the public demonstrations before companies, etc. Have him place a key in a book, under a rug, back of a picture, and in similar difficult places. Let him exercise his ingenuity in finding strange places in which to hide the object. In the experiments in finding the hidden objects he must train himself to give you the mental messages "up"; "down"; "to the right"; "to the left," etc., just as he did his old message or impulse "this way." And you must train yourself to receive them. This training will be of the greatest possible benefit to you when you are called upon later to find objects hidden in people's pockets, etc.

GENERAL REMARKS ON PRACTICE.

The above exercises will train the student to receive and act upon the mental commands or messages of the Transmitter, under a great variety of circumstances and conditions. Many of the most successful public "Mind Readers" started out in public work with far less careful and thorough training. But there are now still greater degrees of proficiency possible. The student will find in succeeding chapters a number of interesting and startling feats and experiments which are intended for parlor audiences, etc., but which may be most profitably practiced previously with the aid of a good friendly Transmitter, in order that the Performer may familiarize himself with the details of the experiment, and thus be more at his ease when he demonstrates it in public. Then other new experiments and feats will suggest themselves from time to time, to the intelligent student which, likewise, should be practiced previous to a public demonstration.

In finding a hidden object, the first thing to do is to get an idea of the direction. Then the general location of the hiding place; and so on, from general impressions to detailed ones, until at last the fingers close upon the object itself. The Transmitter will be greatly relieved when the object is finally found, and the relaxing of his mental tension may be distinctly felt, and then you will know that your search is at an end.

PREPARING FOR PUBLIC WORK.

Before taking you on with the work before an audience, we must urge upon you to prepare yourself thoroughly by means of the above mentioned exercises. The great tendency among students is to hurry through to the public work, and skipping the exercises as much as possible. This is all wrong. You will never be a thoroughly good demonstrator of anything in life, until you master the rudiments, and by practice familiarize yourself thoroughly with the details of the work. And Mind Reading is no exception. It is true that after a few exercises you may be able to give a fair demonstration before an audience, but you will never get further than "fair" without careful practice. And therefore we urge you to have patience and perseverance, and to stick to the exercise until you become a Master of Mind Reading, when you need fear no audience whatsoever, and will be able to give a demonstration that will be a great credit to both yourself and to us, your instructors.

And, now for your work before an audience, remembering, always that the feats and experiments that we shall mention, should be practiced by you privately, with the aid of a friendly Transmitter, before you reproduce them in public. In the case of feats, in which the audience is a party to the experiment, such as the finding of a scarf-pin on a member of the audience, you may practice with a dummy audience, that is with an imaginary audience consisting of chairs, etc., until you familiarize yourself with the details of the feat.

LESSON V.

SIMPLE DEMONSTRATIONS.

In beginning a public demonstration, it will be well for you to give a short preliminary talk to the audience, somewhat along the following lines:

OPENING TALK.

"Ladies and Gentlemen, with your assistance I shall endeavor to give you a demonstration of practical Mind Reading, beginning with some simple feats, and then proceeding gradually to more complicated demonstrations. In these demonstrations, I must have your co-operation, for the success of the experiments depends as much upon you as upon myself. In the first place, I must ask that you refrain from conversation, laughter, etc., while I am demonstrating, for these things distract the mind of the Transmitter and prevent him from concentrating his Mind and Will upon mine; and also prevent me from maintaining that Passive Mental State which is essential to the success of the experiments. I trust that you will help me in this way. I also ask that during the experiments, you will all concentrate your Mind and Will upon me, and help me in the work. In order to obtain the best results all Mind Readers prefer that their audiences concentrate their Wills upon the work, with the purpose of mentally willing that the demonstrator be successful. In fact the success of the experiments depend very materially upon the Willing exerted by the audience. If you Will in my favor, I shall be successful; if you Will that I shall fail, I shall feel the effect. Therefore, kindly give me your aid. I ask you to blindfold me and take such other means to prevent unfair methods and practices, as your judgment may dictate. I am now ready to proceed with the tests."

CHOOSING THE TRANSMITTER.

Then have the audience select a committee to blindfold you and remain outside of the room with you, while the remainder of the audience select the object that you are to find, etc. When you return to the room, select someone to act as Transmitter. If possible get someone with whom you have previously practiced, and established rapport conditions. This will aid you very materially, of course. If this is not possible, select someone of the audience that is in harmony with you, and who will have a strong enough will to give you the vibrations. Sometimes women are very good at this work, as they get very much in earnest when interested, and therefore Will intently. If your first Transmitter is not satisfactory, test another, and so on until you get a good one. You may change Transmitters during the evening, if you prefer; in fact this is a good plan, if you are an adept, for it shows the audience that there is no collusion.

INSTRUCTING THE TRANSMITTER.

You should instruct the Transmitter, along the lines indicated in a previous chapter, i.e. that he must hold the thought of <u>direction</u>, fix his eyes on the chosen spot and then <u>concentrate his will</u> upon it, and that your success will depend materially upon <u>his ability to concentrate his Mind and Will upon the task</u>. You should explain to him that you receive your impulses through his thought-waves or vibrations, and that the stronger these are, the better you will succeed. Make this plain to him. When the Transmitter fails to concentrate his Will, you will know it at once, and should call his attention to it, saying "Concentrate, concentrate now—<u>harder</u>—use your <u>Will</u>," or words to that effect. You should impress upon the Transmitter that it is the <u>strength of his Will</u> that produces the mental vibrations that give you the impressions.

BEGINNING THE TEST.

Then, take the hand of the Transmitter, in the manner already described in previous lesson, placing it to your forehead, or else holding it up high in front of you. Then begin a wavering motion, or direction, preferably describing a circle, slowly. In this meaningless wavering motion remain perfectly passive awaiting impressions. Soon you will begin to feel a mental resistance to certain directions, and a mental willingness that you move in another direction. Then move along the line of the least mental resistance. In some cases you will receive a strong <u>mental urge</u>, <u>pull</u>, or <u>push</u>, in the direction of the selected spot. Here is where your practice comes in, for in your practice experiments you have acquired the art of recognizing these impressions as they come to you, in their different forms, and so are prepared to yield to them and move accordingly. It is impossible to describe in writing just how these impressions come, and feel like, for actual experience is necessary before you will know just what is meant. But once you have accustomed yourself to receive and recognize the impressions, the rest is all a matter of practice and development.

And now for the demonstrations themselves. You should begin with the simplest feats, and then work up gradually to the more complicated and difficult ones. This plan will build up your own powers, and will develop the Transmitter's. We herewith give a number of interesting feats and demonstrations, explaining the details of each. Of course, the general directions we have given regarding the receiving of impressions, etc., will apply to all of these feats, for the principle underlying them all is the same, precisely.

FINDING A LOCATION.

DEMONSTRATION I. Begin by having the audience select a part in the room, which may be easily reached by you. Then proceed as directed, until you feel that you have reached the right place, or location.

FINDING A PERSON.

DEMONSTRATION II. Have the audience select a person, one of their number. Find the general location of the person. Then standing still, reach out your right hand, and begin "feeling about." You will find that as your hand moves away from the right person you will feel a <u>drawing back</u> impression, whereas when you reach toward the person you will receive an <u>urging forward</u> impression. A little practice will soon enable you to distinguish these mental impressions. Then place your hand on the person who seems to be the centre of the impressions. If this is the wrong person, you will receive a mental impression of "<u>Wrong</u>"; in which case you must start up the moving your hand to and fro, and around, until you feel the urge impression, when you should place your hand on the person immediately in front of you. When you reach the right person, you will receive an unmistakable impression and mental message of "All Right," followed by a lessening of the Will tension, and you will know that you have succeeded. You should practice this in private before attempting public demonstration.

FINDING A SMALL OBJECT.

DEMONSTRATION III. Have the audience select some small object in plain sight in the room. Then find it in the manner described of above in the case of the selected person. The rule is identically the same. But there are some other details to be observed, in the matter of "up or down," for the object may be higher than your shoulder or lower, in which case you will have to either reach up or down. In this reaching up or down, follow the same general rule as given. When you reach the right location, you will feel an impression of "not yet finished" from the mind of the Transmitter. Then reach up slowly. If this is right you will receive a corresponding impression, and may go on to centre the object. But if it is not right, you will receive a mental urge <u>downward</u>, which you should follow. The rule always is to <u>follow the line of the least mental resistance</u>. You will always receive the resistance when you are not succeeding, and will always receive the lack of resistance when you are succeeding. Learn to focus these impressions until they centre positively and constantly on the same spot—<u>then you have succeeded</u>, for there will be your object right under your hand.

FINDING A BOOK.

DEMONSTRATION IV. Have the audience select a book on the shelves of a book case, and then find it in the manner just related. The two feats are precisely the same, although the latter will appear more startling to the observer.

THE FLORAL TRIBUTE.

DEMONSTRATION V. This test is known as "The Floral Tribute." It is performed by having a bouquet of flowers on the table. Then select some young man in the audience, and let him pick out some young woman in the audience whom he wishes to have the flowers. You must retire from the room, of course, while he selects the young lady and mentions her name and position to the audience. Then returning to the room, pick up the bouquet, and taking the hand of your Transmitter, find the young lady and present her with the flowers. Of course this feat is merely a fancy rendition of the simple feat of finding the person thought of, and is performed in the same way. (Study the directions for Demonstration II, and apply in the present case, with appropriate variations.)

THE REUNITED COUPLE.

DEMONSTRATION VI. This test is known as "The Reunited Couple." It is performed by having the audience select two persons, a young man and a young woman, and stand them up in front of the room, like a couple about to be married. Then they should have a third person, a man, selected and stood before them as the parson who will tie the knot. The three persons should then take their seats, and when you enter the room, and take the hand of your Transmitter, you must first find "the Parson"; then "the Groom"; and then "the Bride," and arrange them in their proper positions. This is a highly effective test, and invariably brings hearty applause, and the hunt affords much merriment to the audience. But, as you will see readily, it is but a variation of Demonstration II.

THE HIDDEN JEWELRY.

DEMONSTRATION VII. Have the audience select some small article, like a scarf-pin, ring, etc., and hide it on the person of some one of the audience. Then you are to find it. This demonstration combines the features of Demonstration II, and Demonstration III, that is you have first to find the person, as described in Demonstration II, and then the object which is practically a variation of Demonstration III. Study the details of Demonstration III, and practice the present demonstration in private before trying it in public.

THE DISCOVERED COURSE.

DEMONSTRATION VIII. Have a member of the audience walk around the room, following a prescribed course selected by the audience. Have your Transmitter memorize the course accurately, and then you must walk over the same course when you return to the room. This is effective, but is merely a variation of the "Finding the Corner" demonstration.

REPLACING THE PIN.

DEMONSTRATION IX. This is called "Replacing the Pin," and is very effective when properly performed. Have a member of the audience take a pin and insert it in the wall in a spot plainly visible to the audience, not too high up, however—about on the level of your shoulder is best. Then have him withdraw the pin and hide it somewhere in the room. Then when you return to the room, and take the Transmitter's hand, you should first find the pin, (in the manner heretofore described) and then find the place where it had been stuck; then circling your hand around in narrowing circles until you feel the proper impression push the pin home in the spot in which it formerly was driven. This final effort is really merely a modification of "finding the spot," and with a little practice may be easily performed.

THE THEFT DETECTED.

DEMONSTRATION X. This feat is called "The Theft." Have one of the audience play "the thief," and steal an article of jewelry, or similar small object from a second person called "the victim." Then the thief should hide his spoil in a safe place about the room. Returning you first find the thief; then the hidden article; then the person, according to the methods already given. This is a very effective feat, but is merely a combination of "Finding the Person," and "Finding an Object."

THE RECONSTRUCTED TABLEAU.

DEMONSTRATION XI. This feat is known as the "Reconstructed Tableau." It is performed by having several of the audience form a simple tableau group, and then retire to their seats. Returning to the room you are to find each person; lead him or her to the former spot; then reconstruct the group. This is somewhat difficult, but not nearly so much so as you might suppose. A little private practice will enable you to perform it with ease.

THE MURDER AND THE DETECTIVE.

DEMONSTRATION XII. This test is known as the "Murder and the Detective," and is very spectacular and sensational, and is accordingly one that is in great favor with the public performers. It is performed as follows: The audience selects one man to act as the "murderer"; another to act as "the victim"; and also some object to act as the dagger; and lastly a place in which the body is to be concealed. Then the "murderer" picks up the "dagger," and "kills" his "victim," afterward concealing the body in some part of the room (usually sitting in a chair) and the "dagger" in another place. Then when you return to the room you first find the "body"; then the "wound"; then the "dagger," and then the "murderer." This is usually announced as a wonderful piece of "telepathic detective work," and is extremely effective, and may be reserved as the "principal effect" of your series of demonstrations.

You will notice that the feat is merely an elaborate combination of the simpler feats of "Finding the Person," "Finding the Object," etc.

THE RETURNED HATS.

DEMONSTRATION XIII. Have the hats of a number of men in the audience placed on a table or other place, and then returning to the room, blindfolded of course, you pick up the hats, one by one, and place them upon the heads of their proper owners, who are seated in different parts of the room. This is a simple feat although very effective. It is, of course, merely a variation of the feat of "finding the person." There is one point, however, that must be remembered in this feat, and that is that the Transmitter should know just whose hat is held in your hand—just who the owner of that particular hat is and where he is sitting or standing. Otherwise he cannot send you the mental impulses which will enable you to find the owner. It will be well for the Transmitter to hold the hat so that it can be seen by the audience, requesting the owner to rise in his seat so as to indicate his whereabouts—your back being turned to the audience while this is being done in order to avoid suspicion of your "peeping," etc.

THE LADY AND THE RING.

DEMONSTRATION XIV. This feat is performed by having a lady in the audience loan the Transmitter her ring. When you return to the room, you find the lady and replace the ring upon the finger from which she took it. The Transmitter must remember the lady, and the particular finger, of course—the rest is simply a combination of the "finding the person" and "finding the spot" feats. It is very effective, if neatly performed.

GENERAL ADVICE.

I. We have given you a great variety of Demonstrations or Feats, but you must not attempt to produce all of them at an evening's entertainment. It will take some time to perform a few of them effectively, and impressively, and you should avoid any attempt to hurry through the feats. Nor should you spoil your good impression by cheapening the demonstrations in the direction of performing too many at one sitting.

II. Neither should you tire or fatigue yourself by too many feats. When your mind or body are tired, you do yourself an injury to perform these demonstrations, and besides, you cannot obtain the best results while fatigued. You should rest a little while after each feat, before attempting another one.

III. When the entertainment, or exercises are over, you should take a few strong deep breaths, swing your arm around a little to promote the circulation, and relieve the nervous tension. You may feel a little "dazed" at first after performing a few feats, but will soon learn to throw off the passive condition, and engage in the laughing conversation that will follow the entertainment. Do not take yourself too seriously and remember that laughter and a little boyish or girlish spirits is a wonderful tonic.

IV. Do not become impatient if you do not progress as rapidly as you would desire. You are practically developing a sixth sense, and are like a baby learning to walk—it takes time, but practice will surely bring you success. Take things calmly. The feats that will be possible for you to perform, even from the start will be wonderful enough, without any necessity for your complaining about your slowness in learning to perform the more complicated ones.

ABOUT TRANSMITTERS.

I. If your Transmitter does not do his work properly, and you feel that he is not Concentrating properly, or using his Will effectively, do not hesitate to change him. You need not offend him, for you may say simply that the rapport conditions are not fully developed between you, and that these things sometimes happen, etc. Your new Transmitter will feel anxious to do better than his predecessor, and will be most likely to Concentrate and Will to the best of his ability.

II. The Transmitter should be in earnest, and no levity or trifling should be permitted. If you have the selection, pick out some earnest person, and avoid the trifling, feather-brained class.

III. If your Transmitter does not seem to be Concentrating properly, you should speak to him firmly, but kindly, about it. Say to him: "Please concentrate your Mind, and Will earnestly—fix your Mind on the right Spot—make a determined Mental Effort that I move in the right direction—it is your Mind and Will that gives me the impression, remember—it all depends upon you," etc. This will often have the effect of bracing him up to renewed mental activity, and you will notice the improvement at once.

A WORD OF WARNING.

Beginning your entertainment, caution the audience about placing the hidden objects in places that you cannot conveniently touch—such as high up on the wall; under the strings of a piano, etc. Tell them that you can <u>find</u> the article anywhere, but it must be placed so that you can get at it with only ordinary care and work. Some "Smart Alicks" may try to play pranks on you in this way, but discourage same vigorously at the start, informing the audience that this is a scientific test and not a circus. And, remember this, tell them that the article must never be hidden about the Transmitter, for the reason that he is seldom able to think as intently about his own location as about some place away from him. These are the only restrictions that you need make. Caution the Transmitter to guide you away from obstacles over which you might stumble, or which you might overturn. Tell him that you place yourself in his hands for protection, and then endeavor to think no more about the matter, for such thought tends to distract your passivity.

The above feats or demonstrations are all performed along the same general lines as indicated a little further back, and all are capable of being accomplished by anyone of ordinary intelligence, with a little study, care and practice. Practice makes perfect, in Mind Reading as in everything else, remember, so keep at it until you have worn off the rough edges, and have polished up the details of the work. You may vary, improve, add to, the above feats, and may also insert many new ones for yourself as you proceed with your work. Use your inventive faculties.

THE WIRE CONTACT.

A sensational and effective method of performing some of the simpler feats is performed by some public performers, and consists in having a piece of thick wire, about one foot in length grasped by the Receiver's left hand, and by the Transmitter's right hand, instead of the ordinary contact. A little practice will surprise you in the facility in which the impressions are transferred over the wire from the Transmitter to the Receiver. The methods of operation in this case are identical with those employed in the ordinary methods. A wooden "ruler" may be substituted for the wire. Some performers succeed even with a long walking-cane.

THIRD PERSON INTERPOSED.

Another variation is that in which a third person is interposed between the Transmitter and Receiver. Practice along these lines will enable the skilled Mind Reader to receive the impressions as usual, notwithstanding the interposition of the third person. Do not attempt to try these variations until you have thoroughly mastered the ordinary methods.

(The student is here advised to turn to the conclusion of Lesson VI, of this book, and acquaint himself with the "Simpler Method" there described. It may help him in this phase of his work.)

We shall now pass on to the consideration of some of the more complicated or difficult feats of Contact Mind Reading.

LESSON VI.

DIFFICULT DEMONSTRATIONS.

We shall now direct your attention to a class of demonstrations of a rather more complicated order than those related in the last chapter. But even these difficult feats may be rendered comparatively easy of accomplishment by careful practice, and development of receptivity.

PRELIMINARIES.

In these experiments or demonstrations the Transmitter stands by your left side, you grasping the fingers of his right hand in your left hand, and holding as in the case of the former experiments, i.e. either with his hand pressed against your head, or else held out and up, as before described. You receive the impressions in the same way. The following demonstrations may be performed after a little private practice, so as to be shown at a public performance almost as easily as the simpler feats heretofore described.

DISCOVERING THE CARD.

DEMONSTRATION I. Spread a number of cards over the table. Then retiring from the room, have the audience select one card of the number, which the Transmitter must be sure to remember distinctly—that is the Transmitter should remember just <u>where</u> the card is, the <u>position</u> being the important feature, rather than the name of the card. Then taking the Transmitter's hand as above described, you should move your right hand to-and-fro over the table, moving it backward and forward, and in circles. You will soon find that this feat closely resembles the one of the last chapter in which you find small objects; the pin hole, etc. You will soon find that the impressions <u>tend to centre</u> over a certain spot on the table. Begin to lessen your circles and hand movements until you gradually centre over this spot. Then slowly lower your fingers until you touch the card resting on the said spot, when you will be sure that you are right, when you must pick up the card and exhibit it to the audience. The same indications mentioned in the feats of the last chapter will be felt by you. You will feel the "No, no!" impression when you are wrong, and the "That's right" impression when you are moving in the right direction, until at last you will distinctly feel the relaxation of the mental urge, which you will have learned to translate into "Right you are!" when you finally touch the right card. This feat is really no more difficult than the one in which the small object is found, and we have included it in the list of "Difficult Demonstrations" simply because it is practically a "connecting link" between the two classes of demonstration, as you will see as we proceed.

THE CHECKER MOVE.

DEMONSTRATION II. This is akin to the last experiment. Have a checker board arranged by some of the audience who understands the game. Then let some one decide on the next move. Be sure that the Transmitter thoroughly understands the piece to be moved, as well as the place to where it is to be moved. Then, proceeding as above indicated, first find the piece to be moved, and then move it to the proper place. This feat consists of two parts, you will notice. The finding of the piece is like the finding of the card. Then with the piece grasped between your thumb and forefinger, make a small circular and backward and forward movement, until you feel the mental impression of "There!" when you will place your piece directly on the spot. This may seem difficult, and appears so to the audience, but you will find by a little private practice that it is really as easily performed as some of the simpler tests.

THE GAME OF CARDS.

DEMONSTRATION III. Similar to the above is the feat known as the "Game of cards." Two players sit opposite each other at a table, having dealt themselves two hands of euchre. Have the Transmitter lead you behind the first player, and standing there have the player silently point out the card he wishes to lead, to the Transmitter. The Transmitter then should concentrate his mind on the card, and you will find it in the usual manner, and having found it will play it on the table. Then leading you around to the other player, the Transmitter repeats the process, and you find and play the card. Then back to the first play, and repeat. Then alternate between the players, in the same manner, until you have played out the game. This may be improved upon by the Transmitter thinking of which player has won the trick, when you will push the cards over to the winner, having discovered the direction in the usual manner. This feat is very effective indeed when properly performed.

THE MAPPED-OUT TRIP.

DEMONSTRATION IV. Have a map laid open on the table, and have the audience decide upon a trip between two points, either by rail or by water. Then returning to the room, stand as above described, and with your forefinger find the place from which the trip starts. Then move slowly along the selected course in the same manner in which the checker-game was played, passing along the chosen route until the end is reached. These feats are all really variations of the one principle.

THE PACK OF CARDS.

DEMONSTRATION V. This is a very effective feat, and requires some little skill and practice, but there is no reason why any careful, patient, and persistent student should not be able to master it. It consists in the audience selecting any given card from the pack, and then replacing it with the others, being sure that the Transmitter is familiar with the card chosen, and knows enough about cards to recognize it when he sees it again. Then the pack of cards should be placed on the table, face up. Returning to the room, you take the Transmitter's hand as usual, and with your right hand pick off the cards from the pack, slowly and one by one. As you pick up each card, slowly <u>weigh</u> it in your hand, so to speak, and then place it aside if you receive no "stop" orders from the mind of the Transmitter. Having previously practiced this feat in private you will have learned that peculiar "heavier" sensation that comes to you when you lift the right card from the pack, so that when you finally reach it you will know it. We cannot describe just what this sensation will feel like—you must learn it by actually experiencing it in private practice. We advise you to diligently practice this feat in private, for it is wonderfully effective. You will find that after a bit of practice you will be able to get the "heavy" feeling when you lift up and "weigh" the right card. You should perform this feat slowly, and carefully, shaking your head, "No," just before you discard a card. If by the lack of concentration of the Transmitter, you fail to feel the "heavy" feeling when you pick up the right card, the shake of the head will be apt to arouse him to exert his <u>Will</u> more actively, and you will receive the "hold on" impulse immediately. Do not be in too much of a hurry to discard, but make several feints at it before finally letting go. This feat may be improved by having the audience select a "poker-hand," such as a "flush," a "straight," "three-of-a-kind"; a "full-house," etc., etc., and having you find the hand one card at a time. This latter is a fine effect, and always brings down the house. But be sure that your Transmitter really knows and remembers the cards, else the feat will fail, of course. He must remember each card, and recognize it when it appears face up on the pack before you, as you proceed with the discarding. Never attempt this feat in public without previous careful, private, practice, for it requires the most delicate perception and skill. If you find that you cannot master it to your satisfaction, after sufficient practice, you may try it by the "Simpler Method" given at the conclusion of this Lesson.

THE CHOSEN WORD IN THE BOOK.

DEMONSTRATION VI. Like the last feat, this is a complex and difficult one, but one that always arouses enthusiasm in an audience when well performed. It will repay you for the private practice that you will have to employ upon it, before you produce it in public. The feat consists of the audience selecting a book from a pile, or a book-shelf, or book-case, etc.—then a given page is chosen—then a line of printed matter on that page—and then a <u>word</u> in that line. It is well to have the Transmitter draw a pencil circle around the chosen word, so that he may be sure to remember it later. The book is then replaced on the shelf. Then returning to the room, you first find the book, by the methods already given in previous feats; then laying it flat on the table you should begin to slowly and deliberately pick each leaf up separately. This part of the feat is almost identical with the last one, in which you picked up the cards from the pack. When you get the proper impression, you should announce that you have found the leaf. If satisfied that you are right, ascertain upon which side of the leaf, the chosen page is. This can be done by pressing the leaf to the right, or left, in succession, until you get the right impression as to which way to press it down. Then, having thus found the page, pass your finger slowly down and back over the page several times, until you get the impression of a <u>centre</u>. This centre will be the chosen line. Then by passing the finger slowly along the line, you will discover the Word when you reach it. This is a "ticklish" feat, but it may be mastered by practice—in fact some people have found it almost as simple as some of the easier feats, while others require careful practice with it. Do not be discouraged if you do not succeed at first trial, even in public, but try again, and after a bit you will seem to "get the knack" all at once, and thereafter will have but little trouble in making the demonstration. If you find that you do not meet with the desired degree of success in this feat, try it by the "Simpler Method" given at the last of this part of the book. But do not give it up without the proper practice. If you have carefully performed the previous feats, you should have so developed yourself by this time that you should have no special difficulty in this feat.

BLACKBOARD DEMONSTRATIONS.

The following feats may be performed either upon a large blackboard hanging from the wall, or upon a large sheet of card-board, or stiff paper, spread upon the table. If the blackboard is used, you should stand before it, the Transmitter standing in the usual position. If the table is used, you should stand before it, the Transmitter in his usual place.

DRAWING THE CHOSEN FIGURE.

DEMONSTRATION VII. Have the audience select a number, and think intently of it. Impress upon the Transmitter that is to think of the <u>Shape</u> of the figure instead of merely remembering its name. For instance if the figure "8" is thought of, the Transmitter should think of the <u>Shape</u> of the figure, and not of the word "eight." Then begin to circle your hand around over the blackboard just as you did when finding the place of the "beginning of the trip" of the demonstration mentioned a few minutes ago.

Then bring your pencil or chalk to a starting point, which you will soon perceive. Then hold your fingers pressing lightly forward, and impart to your hand a trembling vibratory motion as if in hesitation regarding the next movement, saying at the same time to your Transmitter: "<u>Will Hard</u> now—<u>Will</u> the <u>Direction</u> to me," and you will soon begin to get an impression of "Right," or "Left," or "Down," as the case may be, which you should follow slowly. Be slow about it, for if the impression is not right you will soon be checked up. Fence around a little until you begin to get the impressions clearly. You will find that the principal trouble is at the start, for once you are started on the right track, your Transmitter's Will will be freely employed, and he will pour the impressions into you. Let him feel that it is <u>his Will</u> that is really doing the work, and he will exert it freely. Once started, these drawing feats are easily performed, the trouble being with the start. You should practice this feat frequently in private, before attempting it in a public demonstration. It is very effective.

THE LADY'S AGE.

DEMONSTRATION VII. This is a variation of the above feat. A lady in the audience is asked to whisper her age in the ear of the Transmitter, and you are to draw it on the board or paper. The feat is performed precisely in the manner described above, the Transmitter being cautioned to think of but <u>one figure at a time during the drawing</u>.

THE BANK NOTE TEST.

DEMONSTRATION IX. Akin to the last two feats, is the reading of the number of a bank-note held in the hand of the Transmitter. It is performed in precisely the same manner as the preceding feat. Be sure to have the Transmitter understand that he is to think of but one figure at a time, until it is drawn, and then the next, and so on.

THE WATCH NUMBER TEST.

DEMONSTRATION X. The feat of reading and drawing the number of a person's watch is a variation of the last mentioned demonstration, and is performed in precisely the same way.

THE GEOMETRICAL FIGURE TEST.

DEMONSTRATION XI. Have the audience select some simple geometrical figure, such as a square, triangle, circle, right angle, etc., and proceed to draw it in the same way as the figures in the demonstrations just described. Have the Transmitter hold the figure in his mind and <u>mentally draw it</u> as you proceed. A little private practice will enable you to draw these figures easily, and in fact, they are really simpler than numbers, although more startlingly effective at times.

DRAWING PICTURES.

DEMONSTRATION XII. The same principle described in the above mentioned test may be extended to apply to the drawing of simple pictures, such as the outline figure of a pig, etc. The copy is placed on the table or blackboard, so that the Transmitter may easily refer to it, and then you proceed as in the feats above mentioned. Practice this until you "get it down fine."

THE HIDDEN NAME.

DEMONSTRATION XIII. The same principle may be extended to the writing down of the name of a person, town, etc., previously chosen by the audience. Draw in large letters, so that the eye of the Transmitter may easily follow you at each step.

THE UNDERLYING RULE.

In all of the "Drawing Demonstrations," you should remember the primary principle, i.e. Follow the line of the least Mental Resistance, and the Will of the Transmitter will invariably lead you to the right direction.

THE "SIMPLER METHOD."

A simpler method of performing the feats and demonstrations which we have styled "The More Difficult Feats," is that of having the Transmitter stand by your right side, turning toward you and placing his right hand over yours, the tips of his fingers resting on your fingers between your large knuckles and first joints, (instead of standing on your left side with his fingers grasped in your left hand, as heretofore mentioned). This method is not nearly so good so far as appearances go, for some critical members of the audience might object that he was in confederacy with you and really helping you to draw—but it is highly effective so far as simplifying the feat is concerned. His finger-tips with their nervous matter aroused into activity seem to fairly charge your fingers with "nervous energy," or "magnetism," and your hand acts almost automatically. The motion of the Receiver's hand and fingers, under this method becomes almost like the motion of a "Planchette," and often writes and draws the numbers, figures, letters, etc., so easily and smoothly, that they seem to be fairly "running away" from the mind of the performer. You should at least familiarize yourself with this method, so as to be able to use it in emergencies, or in the case of a poor Transmitter, or else in the case of the more delicate and complex tests. If you neglect this method, you will have failed to acquaint yourself with one of the most startling features of Contact Mind Reading, which so far touches the higher phenomena that it is closely akin to what is known as "Automatic Writing." In fact, if you are disposed, and are naturally receptive and sensitive to impressions, you may even write a letter through the <u>Will</u> of a good Transmitter, by this method. By all means make yourself acquainted with its possibilities, and phenomena.

We now pass on to a consideration of the more Sensational Feats.

LESSON VII.

SENSATIONAL FEATS.

In addition to the feats given in this work, which, together with their countless variations, form the stock in trade of the majority of the professional Mind Readers, there are a number of other feats essayed by the public performers which we have seen fit to group under the general title "Sensational Feats." These feats are described here in order that the student may understand the nature of them, and the manner of their performance. But we consider such feats suitable only for the sensational advertisements of the professional performers, and always dependent upon more or less spectacular accessories, and attended by even dangerous features in the case of the driving feat. And therefore we do not offer them for reproduction by the private student, or the parlor demonstrator. The principal Sensational Feats performed by the professionals, are as follows:

THE DRIVING FEAT.

This is performed by the performer, blindfolded as usual, driving a team along the public streets to some selected point, which point is usually a hotel previously selected by a public committee. Upon reaching the hotel the performer goes to the hotel register, turns the pages and finds a name previously selected. The performer receives his impressions from members of the committee who are seated beside him on the carriage seat, with their arms on his shoulders, or having hold of his hands, or even connected with him by wire. The feat is really a spectacular reproduction of the familiar feats described in previous chapters, and the principles governing it are precisely the same. The Transmitters impress the direction upon him, and he follows the line of the Least Mental Resistance.

THE COMBINATION LOCK FEAT.

This feat is employed either separately, or in connection with the Driving Feat. It consists in the performer opening the combination safe of a hotel or some business establishment. In this case the Transmitter must know the combination perfectly, and his mental impressions acting upon the performer give him the cue to turn "right" or "left" or "repeat" as the case may be. Of course one must have cultivated a great degree of sensitiveness to mental impressions before he will be able to receive and respond to the direction impressions in this case. And yet almost any person by following the directions given in this work, and carefully and repeatedly practicing the various feats and demonstrations given herein, may be able to reproduce this feat of the professional performer, who is in constant daily practice, and who is able to devote his entire time to the work, as his "bread and butter" is concerned therein. Once the sensitiveness is gained, the details of the work are nothing more than those employed in any of the "finding" or "drawing" feats herein described and explained.

THE OFFICE DETECTIVE FEAT.

In this feat the public committee picks out an object on the desk, or about the office of some one of its members, the office being located some distance from the place of meeting. The performer then rushes along the public streets, dragging the Transmitter with him, until the office is reached, then up stairs, and into the room selected, and up to the desk, or other place, and lo! the object is found. Divesting this feat of all its sensational features, the student will see that it is merely a variation of the ordinary "finding" feat performed in the parlor. It creates a great sensation, but there is nothing more wonderful about it than about the simplest "finding" feat.

THE POSTOFFICE FEAT.

Another feat favored by some of the professional performers is that of having a letter placed in a post-office lock-box, the key of which is given the performer at a point some distance from the post-office. Rushing through the public streets, dragging the Transmitter with him, the performer finds the post-office in the usual way, and then locates the lock-box, into which he inserts the key and extracts the letter, thus triumphantly completing the feat. This feat, as every student will see, is merely a variation of the simpler feats manifested in a sensational manner for the purpose of public advertisement.

THE FIRE-ALARM FEAT.

This feat is another "free advertisement" demonstration, in which the performer, with the permission of the city officials, discovers the location of a certain fire-alarm box, and turns on the alarm with the key which had been previously loaned him. Some public officials allow this test to be performed, using it as a test alarm for the department as well, and the sight and sound of the clanging fire-engines, the smoke, and confusion following upon the sensational Mind Reading demonstration is calculated to cause great excitement and interest in the town, which usually results in packed houses at the night entertainment. But the test is really nothing but a variation of the simple "finding the spot" demonstration, with sensational accompaniments.

VARIATIONS.

We might enlarge our list of "Sensational feats," but to no real benefit to the student, for they are all cut from the same cloth, and are but "improvements" upon the simple parlor feats. If the student wishes to do so, he may invent a dozen similar feats, just as sensational and just as effective. The purpose of the sensational feat is primarily to gain free advertisements for the public performers. As scientific demonstrations they have but very slight value.

"FAKE DEMONSTRATIONS" EXPOSED.

In concluding this part of the book, we wish to warn our students against some of the so-called "Mind Readers" who are travelling around the country giving exhibitions of so-called Mind Reading which while interesting enough in themselves are nothing but cleverly devised devices intended to counterfeit the genuine phenomena. The majority of these performers have a series of cleverly arranged "signal-codes" by which the confederate conveys to the "Mind Reader" the name and description of the article handed to the former by some one of the audience. One of the principal performers in this line in this country had a signal-code of over five-thousand objects, which he and his confederate had carefully memorized. This code was worked by the plan of asking the blindfolded "Mind Reader" to name the object. You can see the possibilities of this when you remember the many different ways in which the same question may be asked, and when you remember that each word, and combination of words, conveys a distinct and separate meaning to the blindfolded one.

Others employ sleight-of-hand, and legerdemain, in order to produce the illusion. Prepared pads of paper upon which questions are written, and similar means, are commonly used in such exhibitions. We do not purpose going into this matter in detail, for such is not the purpose of this work. But we think it well to call the attention of our students to the same, in order that they may get a clue to some of the various counterfeit exhibitions of Mind Reading which are being advertised by some of the public performers. There are other public performers, however, who give fine exhibitions of the genuine phenomena. The student of this work should have acquired a sufficient knowledge of its underlying principles to enable him to distinguish between the genuine and the spurious when he sees an exhibition. If any wish to know more of the counterfeit, there are many good works published on "Legerdemain" which will satisfy his curiosity.

LESSON VIII.

HIGHER PHENOMENA.

In the demonstrations described and explained in the previous parts of this work, the mental impressions travel from one mind to another over the channels of the "telegraphic wires" of the nervous system of the Transmitter and Receiver. In other words the Mind Reading that is employed in the feats and demonstrations given, is akin to the ordinary "telegraphic current" travelling over the wires from sending station to receiving station—the nervous system of the two persons furnishing a very close counterpart to the telegraphic wire, etc. But there is a step beyond this—many steps in fact. While the "Contact Mind Reading" which we have described and explained is surely wonderful enough to attract the attention of all thinking minds, still when the advanced student passes on to the field of the Higher Phenomena he is destined to meet with marvelous results which in some cases almost surpass belief. This Higher Phenomena of Mind Reading, or "Telepathic Mind Reading," when compared to the Contact Mind Reading, is as the "wireless telegraph" when compared to the ordinary telegraph using wires.

In Lesson I, of this book, we have given you the theories held by scientific men regarding the nature of the waves or currents that proceed from one mind to another, and the mechanism by which these waves are registered. We think it will be interesting to many of you to know that certain Occultists have their own theory regarding this matter, which while not widely known is still of the greatest interest to earnest students of the scientific side of the subject. We allude to what is known as "The Pineal Gland" theory.

The Pineal Gland is a small gland, cone-shaped, and of a reddish-gray color, situated in the brain about the middle of the skull, nearly above the top of the spinal column. It is a compact mass of nervous matter, containing a quantity of what has been called "brain-sand," which is composed of very small particles of gritty matter. The anatomists and physiologists confess their ignorance of the function and purpose of the Pineal Gland, and it remains for the Occultists to explain its real nature, which is the receiving and registering of the waves or currents, or vibrations of thought and Will received from another person. This Pineal Gland is, according to the Occultists, the receiving instrument for the "wireless Mind Reading," and in fact it resembles the actual receiver of the wireless telegraph in more than one respect.

THE FIRST STEPS.

In the first place, the student who is practicing the experiments given in previous chapters, and who is making the demonstrations given there, will find that at times he is able to do away with the physical contact. He will loosen his hold upon the hand of the Transmitter, and at times will sever the contact entirely, and after the feat is demonstrated he will realize to his astonishment that he has performed the principal part of the feat without contact at all. He may be almost unconscious of this fact, for the reason that he was so much immersed and absorbed in his work that he did not have time to think of these details. At other times he will find that even before he has made the physical contact with the Transmitter, he will receive a flash of mental impression which will enable him to proceed to the selected location, or object, at once.

DEMONSTRATIONS WITHOUT A TRANSMITTER.

These experiences will become so frequent and so strong that he may often (in the cases of peculiarly sensitive people) perform the entire feat without the physical contact of the Transmitter, and perhaps without any Transmitter at all. In well developed cases the Receiver may perform the simple feats, and sometimes some of the more complicated ones, merely by the aid of the Concentrated Will of the audience.

We have known of cases in which a pocket-knife was the selected and hidden object, and when the demonstrator would enter the room he would receive a sudden mental impression of the word "knife," followed by the impression "under the sofa-pillow," etc., and upon going to the designated spot the knife would be found. Every person who carefully practices the demonstrations given in this book will be able to add actual experiences of this kind, of his own, which have been experienced by him during the course of his work.

In order to develop the ability to produce the Higher Phenomena, the best course is for the student to frequently practice the demonstration and experiments of Contact Mind Reading, as this will develop the receptive faculties of the mind. Then the student may occasionally practice with a few sympathetic and harmonious friends, endeavoring to reproduce the demonstrations without physical contact.

EXERCISES FOR DEVELOPMENT.

He may also try the experiment of having a friend hold a certain number of small buttons, etc., in his hand, and endeavor to <u>will</u> that the student shall "guess" the right number. Some people attain a surprising proficiency in this work, almost from the first. A similar experiment with the pack of cards, the student endeavoring to "guess" the card drawn from the pack, naming color, suit, and number in turn, may afford successful results. A number of these experiments may be thought of by an ingenious person, remembering always that the "guess" is not a guess at all, but an attempt to register the mental impression of the Transmitter.

REPRODUCING THE SPERRY FEATS.

The student may with great profit endeavor to reproduce the experiments of the Sperry children related in Lesson II of this work, in our account of the experiments of the Society for Psychical Research.

THE WILLING GAME.

The well-known "Willing Game" will afford you an opportunity to develop this faculty of "wireless" Mind Reading. Your audience is seated in the room, and you enter blindfolded. An object has been previously selected. You stand in the centre of the room, and the audience wills "to the right"; then "forward"; then "a little lower down," etc., etc., etc., until the object is found, just as was the case when the Transmitter sends the impressions. The audience should Will <u>only one step at a time</u>, and you should take that one step without thought of the succeeding ones. The mind should be held as receptive as possible, that is "open" to vibrations. Take your time, and do not let hurry or anxiety enter your mind. It will be well to practice this experiment with members of your family, or with harmonious and sympathetic friends.

LONG DISTANCE EXPERIMENTS.

Experiments of "wireless" Mind Reading or Telepathy may be tried between friends at long distances, space apparently presenting no obstacle to the passage of the thought waves. Pick out some friend with whom you have established a strong <u>rapport</u> condition by means of his having acted as your Transmitter in your Contact Mind Reading experiments, and by having practiced Rhythmic Breathing, as heretofore described. Have the Transmitter sit in his room at the appointed time, gazing intently at some small simple object, such as a knife, a glass, a cup, a book, etc., and endeavoring to make <u>a clear mental picture of it</u>, which picture he should also <u>Will</u> to be reproduced in your mind. Remember he should think of the looks or appearance of the object not merely of its name—he should think of the shape, etc., of the book, instead of thinking the word "book." At the same time you should sit quietly in your room, placing yourself in the same passive, receptive mental attitude that you have acquired and practiced in your Contact Mind Readings. Then wait patiently for impressions. After a while, if successful, you will get the <u>mental picture</u> of a book, or whatever object was thought of by the Transmitter. This experiment may be varied from time to time, the principle being the same in all cases. It will be well for both the Transmitter and the Receiver to keep a written record of the time of each experiment, and the objects thought of. Several objects may be thought of at a sitting of say five minutes apart, a careful record being kept by both parties of the time, and object, so that a later comparison may show the result of the experiments. In case of the two people being in different cities, they may mail each other copies of their record for comparison.

THE "AUTOMATIC WRITING" EXPERIMENTS.

Another way of conducting experiments along the lines of the Higher Phenomena of Mind Reading, is akin to the "Automatic Writing" known to all students of Occultism. The Transmitter concentrates his thought and Will in the usual manner, while the Receiver places himself in the usual receptive, passive state of mind, and awaits the impressions. But instead of the Receiver merely sitting as usual, he draws his chair to a table, having a soft pencil in his hand and a pad of paper on the table before him. He holds the pencil lightly between his fingers, with its point touching the paper—and then awaits impressions. Under good conditions, after waiting a time the pencil will begin to twitch and move feebly. The hands and fingers should allow it full and free motion. After a few moments of indecision the pencil will often begin to write out words. In many experiments <u>the word, or object thought of by the Transmitter will be written out, or drawn in full by the hand of the Receiver</u> acting automatically. Some experimenters succeed much better with this plan than with the more common method.

THE STEAD EXPERIMENTS.

Mr. W.T. Stead, the well-known London editor and investigator of Psychic Phenomena, discovered this method while he was experimenting along the lines of Automatic Writing from disembodied souls. He found that he was really coming in contact with the thought-waves emanating from the minds of the living, instead of the dead. He persisted in his experiments along these lines, and after a time was able to write out full letters embodying the thoughts in the minds of persons of his acquaintance, and others. Other investigators have reproduced his experiments with marvelous results. There is a great field here, awaiting investigation, and it may be that some of the students of this work are destined to add to the scientific testimony on the subject. The above simple directions are all that are necessary, in order to conduct this scientific experiment.

RAPPORT CONDITIONS.

There is a great difference in the degrees of rapport existing between different people, and as the degree of success depends upon the degree of rapport, it is of the greatest importance that you find some person with whom you are in harmonious vibration, in order to try these experiments in the Higher Phenomena.

We will not burden the student with recitals of experiments to perform in this Higher Phenomena demonstration. He may readily devise experiments for himself, from the examples given in connection with the Contact Mind Reading. The Transmitter may think of a card; an object; a name; a place; a scene; a thought; a feeling, etc., etc., without limit. And it makes no difference in the nature of the experiment or test, whether it be tried at long-range, or in the same room, without contact. The feat is the same—the principle is the same.

THE BLACKBURN-SMITH EXPERIMENTS.

As a further suggestion to the student, we would refer him to Lesson II of this work, to the report of the experiments with Mr. Smith and Mr. Blackburn. If you will carefully read this report again, you will find a wealth of suggestions regarding the forms of demonstrations. But, bless your hearts, the experiments may be varied without end—the principle is the same in each case. The underlying principle is that the Transmitter thinks intently upon the appearance of the object or thing, or else upon the feeling connected with it if it be a feeling instead of an object; and the Receiver endeavors to receive the impression. The Transmitter manifests an Active <u>Will</u> to transmit the mental image, while the Receiver assumes a passive, receptive <u>desire</u> to receive the impression. The one is all <u>Will</u>—the other is all <u>Desire</u>.

Concluding this chapter on the Higher Phenomena of Mind Reading, we would say to the students that very few of them will have the perseverance to continue their experiments beyond the point of Contact Mind Reading, or perhaps the simplest forms of the Higher Phenomena. Contact Mind Reading is far more satisfactory to the average person, for its results are very constant indeed, and comparatively little labor, time and trouble are necessary to make the demonstrations. While on the contrary the results of the demonstrations of the Higher Phenomena are less constant except in the cases of very highly developed Receivers, working with Transmitters in almost perfect <u>rapport</u> and harmony. Then the average experiments along the lines of the Higher Phenomena, some days will prove highly successful, while other days will be almost barren of result. In fact there seems to be a sort of spontaneous action in the production of the Higher Phenomena, and the degree of success depends more or less upon some <u>conditions</u> of the mental world, not as yet fully understood by science. But to those who wish to push into the Unknown as far as they may do so, this field of the Higher Phenomena of Mind Reading offers a fascination and attraction difficult to express to those who have not experienced it.

FINIS.

Milton Keynes UK
Ingram Content Group UK Ltd.
UKHW012315040624
443649UK00007B/646